WINK

Transforming Public Speaking with Clown Presence

By Don Colliver

To request permissions, contact the publisher at info@doncolliver.com

Paperback: ISBN: 979-8-9862767-0-0
Hardcover: ISBN: 979-8-9862767-3-1
eBook: ISBN: 979-8-9862767-1-7
Audiobook: ISBN: 979-8-9862767-2-4

First paperback edition June 2022

Published by Colliver Communications

www.collivercommunications.com

TABLE OF CONTENTS

WINK

INTRODUCTION

Imagine the best presentation you've ever seen. Really replay it in your mind. Visualize how the presenter had you completely engaged from intro to conclusion. Consider the elements of the presentation that really nailed you, the elements that made you scoot forward in your chair, and the elements that brought a tear to your eye and made your breath catch. Consider the elements that made you want to listen, understand, and maybe even have a drink with the presenter, even if you disagreed with what they had to say.

Those elements attracted you because that presenter created an authentic, dynamic connection with your in-the-moment needs as an audience member. Even though the presenter was the only person speaking, that presentation had turned into a conversation. As an audience member, you felt heard. You felt seen. You felt validated. I call the magic that the presenter used to awaken that feeling Clown Presence. I've successfully used this magic to emotionally and effectively engage audiences of thousands for over two decades at diverse venues ranging from international corporate conferences to Toastmasters speaking championships to circus big tops. This book will teach you how to bring this magic to your presentations.

Clown Presence is not what you think. We're not talking about the floppy-shoed, red-nosed, potentially creepy character you may recognize from pop culture. Clown Presence is a heightened, specific state of being, unique to you. Clown Presence springs from courageous vulnerability, confident authenticity, and the joy of connection. Clown Presence will bring about deeper communication and a more authentic connection with your presentation audiences than you've ever thought possible.

Sound Familiar?

Let's take a random hapless presenter. We'll call him Kelly. Kelly has to deliver an internal quarterly team update for his superiors in the morning. He already has too much on his plate to even consider adding in authentic audience connection. Already tossing and turning with anxiety the night before, Kelly is terrified of looking foolish in front of the executives and worried about letting down the team. He is desperate to receive validation yet equally desperate to hide that desperation. This is Kelly's career we're talking about! Driven to relieve these crippling feelings, he drills his presentation over and over in his mind until it becomes utterly sterile and robotic, eventually editing out every aspect that vaguely portrays his personality. Perhaps Kelly has consumed hours of public speaking books and classes, hoping that impersonal techniques and manipulative hacks will bring success.

Once the fateful presentation finally begins, our presenter does his best to simply disappear behind his content, ignoring his audience completely while at the same time praying they won't find fault with his message. Or maybe he takes the opposite tack, desperately trying to win validation, making bad jokes, and frantically trying to engage his disconnected and eventually repulsed audience. This book is here to save Kelly from these problems!

Who This Book Is For

If you've had some basic presenting experience but want to get better, this book is for you. Perhaps, like Kelly, your job requires you to give quarterly updates, or maybe your volunteer position asks for an annual speech, or perhaps your friend wants you to lead a toast at their wedding. Whatever the case, these upcoming presentations are keeping you up at night. Maybe you've taken some public speaking courses, watched some public speaking videos, or read some public speaking books. You may have even hired a public speaking coach, asking for tough feedback because, hey, you can take it!

This book is different. Clown Presence is a complete change in mindset. The elements of Clown are not tactical techniques or persuasive hacks to allow you to manipulate your audience into accepting your argument more efficiently. This book explains how to attain a complete paradigm shift in your public speaking, beginning by building the faith that you already have what you need to connect with your audience successfully. You just need to uncover it.

The Five P's of Clown Presence

To enable this discovery, I've organized the elements of Clown Presence as they apply to public speaking into the five P's: Personal Confidence, Preparation, Partnership, (im)Perfection, and Play. The best presentations are built on a foundation of *Personal*

Confidence in yourself as a presenter. You reinforce that confidence through rigorous *Preparation*. Confident and prepared, you can go before your audience and develop an authentic *Partnership* with them.

Once your presentation begins, you will find yourself effortlessly moving from point to point, skillfully incorporating *(im)Perfection* in a way that supports your message, all while staying in courageously vulnerable connection with your audience. You will find yourself actually enjoying this real-time conversation with your audience, as will they, because you have begun to add elements of *Play*. "You versus them" will disappear and you will find that you are all working together towards a mutually created understanding of your message.

Now Is the Time

This transformative shift is now more critical than ever. As more and more public speakers are caught in dishonesty and manipulation, we are desperate for truth. Disposable social media and fake news have created an inauthentic and untrustworthy environment that desperately needs authentic and honest communication. Nothing less than a profound shift in the value of authenticity will save our public discourse. Right now, we have the opportunity to make communication more trustworthy, powerful, and effective, one presentation at a time.

And on top of that, as communication progressively shifts to the virtual medium and more work becomes hybrid, authentic communication is becoming even more challenging. These Clown elements will enable greater authenticity and effectiveness in the world of virtual presentations as well.

Our goal here is to uncover these elements of Clown Presence in your public speaking. You will transform into a more effective and joyful communicator, utilizing courageous vulnerability that's authentic, not manipulative. You will embody and use the transformative power of Clown Presence to more deeply connect with your audience and more successfully communicate your message.

Chapter One:

WHAT IS CLOWN?

Before we begin transforming your public speaking with Clown Presence, a bit of background will be helpful. The idea of the Clown goes back far before today's silly circus buffoons and creepy pop culture icons. Clowns have been making us laugh and see our world from a different point of view since the ancient civilizations of Egypt, Rome, and Greece. There has always been an eager audience to watch brave performers courageous enough to reflect the truth of human existence and transform the ordinary into the extraordinary.

Some Native American cultures respected sacred Clown-types in their societal hierarchies. For example, the Sioux of the Great Plains of North America honored what they called the heyoka.[1] Priests and Clowns were often interchangeable societal roles within cultures, sometimes even held by the same person. Court jesters played the Clown role in the Middle Ages, speaking truth to power under the protection of play and cleverness. Even Shakespeare used Clown characters in his plays to innocently reveal the truth of what was going on. Around the sixteenth century, the Commedia Dell'Arte, Italy's form of popular theater, brought forth the archetypal, acrobatic Clown character known as Harlequin, and in the seventeenth century, France created the wistful Clown character of Pierrot, adding in the familiar white face makeup.

Clowns found their way into the circus, where we find the floppy-shoed, bumbling goof so well known today. The broad, colorful face makeup so intimately associated with today's circus Clown was initially intended as a tool to enable communication of subtle facial expressions over large, auditorium-size distances.

Always reflecting society's humanity and transforming the banal into the transcendent, Clowns continued into vaudeville, television, and film, bringing us beloved performers including Charlie Chaplin, Lucille Ball, and Sacha Baron Cohen. Across the ages, these Clowns reflected to their audiences the truth of human existence with generosity and play, making them laugh with empathy and recognition. Clowns encourage us to see life differently, with presence, connection, and hope. This book will help you use these Clown elements to transform your presentations.

Clown Concepts

French physical theater teacher Jacques Lecoq further defined the idea of Clown at his Paris school, École Internationale de Théâtre Jacques Lecoq, founded in 1956. Lecoq explained that the Clown actually requires an authentic connection to the audience to exist. This connection is a two-way conversation created through the Clown's playfulness, togetherness, and openness. This dialogue allows the Clown and their audience to go on a mutually created journey, discovering the twists and turns of the performance together. Finding joy in these back-and-forth patterns is at the heart of adding Clown Presence to your presentations. It allows pleasure in delivering your content and, more importantly, in the actual connection with your audience. This joy is where Clown Presence truly differentiates itself from standard public speaking.

A few explanations of Clown terms can set the stage for understanding how Clown Presence fits into presentations. While this deep level of engagement and connection is common in the realm of

Clown, it can seem revolutionary in the realm of public speaking. Hence, the world of Clown has refined these elements of active connection into the concepts of *le jeu*, *complicité*, and *clin d'œil*.

Le Jeu

The term *le jeu* (pronounced luh-*zhoo*) is French for "the game." With *le jeu*, your presentation comes to life because you are responding spontaneously to the audience, rather than simply repeating a memorized plan. But beyond merely responding, *le jeu* requires that you find pleasure in this constant response. You must discover the deep joy available in immediate human connection. *Le jeu* can make a presentation feel vital, dynamic, and alive because it reminds your audience that the presentation is happening in the moment. *Le jeu* doesn't necessarily mean a literal back-and-forth dialogue during a presentation, but it does mean embodying a responsive, positive awareness towards the audience from moment to moment. We'll explore *le jeu* more deeply in the chapter on Personal Confidence.

> " ... the contact the clown has with his public is immediate, he comes to life by playing with the people who are looking at him."[2]

—*Jacques Lecoq*

Complicité

Once you successfully embody *le jeu*, the audience reciprocates by enjoying and participating in the direct connection as well. This relationship is called *complicité* (pronounced kohm-plee-see-*tay*). Before *complicité*, you are working on getting your passive audience to understand your message. After *complicité*, you and your audience actively pursue the same goal: mutually created understanding. Metaphorically, before *complicité*, you and your audience were on opposite sides of the table, looking at a challenge between you. After *complicité*, you and your audience are on the same side of the table, looking at the challenge together.

For example, if you learn of an experience that your audience has had with your topic during your presentation, you can ask them to participate by sharing anecdotes. You have shifted from presenting to the audience to creating with the audience, enabling audience investment and ownership. We'll explore the concept of *complicité* in the chapter on Partnership.

Clin d'œil

Clin d'œil (pronounced *clahn*-doi) is the French word for wink, the title of this book! The wink represents the ultimate expression of Clown Presence in public speaking. After creating shared understanding through *complicité*, you can use the *clin d'œil*, or metaphorical wink to the audience, to introduce simple patterns and disruptions using shared experience. This "inside joke" deepens the bond between you and your audience, enabling fun and play.

The concept of *clin d'œil* works especially well when you and your audience are dealing with an immediate challenge unrelated to your message, like unpleasant weather or unfortunate travel logistics. You could reference this shared challenge occasionally throughout your presentation, perhaps playfully blaming the shared travel challenge for an unrelated problem mentioned in your presentation, like budget or staffing issues. Even though you and your audience know that this is not truly the case, the *clin d'œil*, or metaphorical wink, allows you to use this shared experience to connect and play with your audience. We'll explore the concept of *clin d'œil* in the chapter on Play. For now, it's time to begin our exploration of the five P's of Clown Presence.

Chapter Two:

PERSONAL CONFIDENCE

The epic journey to bring Clown Presence into your public speaking starts on the inside and progressively moves outward. To begin, you must develop your relationship with yourself; then you develop your presentation and, finally, you develop your connection with the audience. With each step, you reveal more and more of yourself to your audience, becoming more and more vulnerable. That takes confidence. Sound scary? You bet it is!

According to the National Institute of Mental Health, public speaking anxiety affects about 73 percent of the population, nearly three out of every four people.[3] Well-known performers, including Andrea

Bocelli, Jennifer Lawrence, and Adele, struggle with stage fright and performance anxiety. You are not alone!

> "I saw… a study that said speaking in front of a crowd is considered the number one fear of the average person… Number two was death… This means to the average person, if you have to be at a funeral, you would rather be in the casket than doing the eulogy."[4]
>
> —*Jerry Seinfeld*

So how can you overcome this pervasive obstacle? By developing the confidence to be vulnerable. Vulnerability can be defined as being exposed to the possibility of being harmed. There aren't many positions more exposed than public speaking, so why on earth would you do this? The answer: Being confident enough to be vulnerable opens the door to genuine audience connection and can eventually generate those elusive elements of warmth and trust.

> " Vulnerability is the birthplace of love, belonging, joy, courage, empathy, and creativity."[5]
>
> —*Brené Brown*

Since vulnerability is inherently risky, our goal here is not to remove risk. Our goal is to feel confident enough to take the risk of being vulnerable. Clowns risk vulnerability every time they enter the stage.

How do they do it? The answer: they have acquired a sense of confidence within themselves—a rock-solid belief that no matter what happens, no matter how imperfect they may be, setbacks will pass and they will be okay. As a result, they are not afraid to be vulnerable. They are not afraid to take risks. They are not afraid to expose their authentic selves. This is true confidence.

Save the Show

I initially learned the value of vulnerability and confidence in my first Clown class. These principles came into sharp focus in one primary, terrifying exercise called "Save the Show." The premise of "Save the Show" is simple. The would-be Clown enters the stage from behind a curtain. The instructor and class (audience) observe. The Clown has one task: they must save the show by eliciting a laugh from the audience without preparation. However, the instructor has directed the audience beforehand to offer absolutely no pity laughter. The Clown must genuinely and organically earn any laughter from the audience. For me, as the would-be Clown, this exercise was utterly terrifying, seemingly impossible, and definitely cringe-inducing.

I remember nervously shaking behind the curtain before my entrance. Anxiety pumped through my veins. *Why am I doing this to myself? What if they don't laugh? What if I'm just inherently not funny?* My lack of confidence caused me to furiously pre-plan ways to manipulate the audience into laughter. Somehow, I forced myself through the curtain and stumbled into the spotlight. I desperately tried to control the audience's reaction so I could receive validation. I gave them everything I had, from bad jokes, to fart noises, to poorly executed pratfalls. All to no avail. Silence. Nothing. Sweat streamed down my face as I tried and failed to elicit any indication of enjoyment from the stone-faced crowd and instructor.

Exhausted, I finally became still. A feeling of failure coursed through my body. I stood for a long moment, taking a breath, releasing my frantic attempts at control. Finally, with nothing left to lose, I got in touch with how I was really feeling. I threw up my hands and desperately and honestly asked, "What do you want?" To my surprise, the entire room suddenly erupted in laughter. Relief swept over me as I realized that revealing my true self had authentically connected to the audience. From that point on, the confidence that this was enough made eliciting laughter much easier.

I became aware that the laughter came from my choice to reveal myself to the audience in that moment. Somehow, through pure exhaustion, I gained the personal confidence to release trying to manipulate the audience to do what I needed and share my vulnerability instead. This acknowledgment of my truth in the moment created an authentic and powerful connection and surprisingly attained the goal of the exercise. Energy surged through my body. Authenticity was enough to make a connection! I didn't have to be clever! I could trust my authentic, imperfect self!

Everything changed. The audience's laughter had endorsed my vulnerability and given me the confidence to drop my futile attempts at control.

Imagine if I had emerged onto the stage already realizing that I didn't have to wow the audience with incredible feats of humor, realizing that authenticity and confidence were enough. Instead of feeling terrified, I would have felt excited. I would have felt comfortable. And I would have made them laugh.

That is the power of confidence, the inner faith that your authentic self is enough. While what your audience thinks about you and your message is important, what you think about yourself must come first. Counterintuitively, trying to make the audience like you more will actually make them like you less. You may remember this dynamic from grade school. The harder someone tried to be liked the less likable they became.

Dealing with a Hostile Audience

As a public speaker, inevitably you will have to speak to an audience that does not like you for some reason. You may have to deliver some unfortunate news to a team or explain an unpopular policy to a group of employees. This situation is uncomfortable and it's easy to focus on trying to win your audience over and end up neglecting your message and possibly alienating your audience even more. In these situations, it's critical to accept what you cannot control (your audience's feelings) and instead focus on what you can control (how you feel about yourself). A presenter must first feel enough within themselves and release the desperate need for audience validation. Ironically, this will often get your audience on your side, even if they don't end up buying into your message.

Feeling enough is how to begin building an equal partnership with your audience, with each side taking responsibility for themselves. Confidence changes the entire dynamic of your interactions with an audience. Authentic confidence is the super-power at the heart of Clown Presence.

A Foundation of Personal Confidence

But how do you build this confidence without braving the terrifying gauntlet of "Save the Show"? Creating a foundation of confidence must happen step by step through small, easy shifts rather than one massive transformation. You establish personal confidence by realizing that you are enough, finding the joy of connection, and adopting a growth mindset.

You Are Enough

Building a foundation of confidence first requires accepting that, whatever happens, you are enough. You must work to believe in yourself as inherently okay as a human being regardless of external validation. Believing that you are enough is the opposite of insecurity. It means realizing you already have everything you need within you, regardless of what happens during your presentation.

This belief is the reason why external validation is inessential. While encouragement and positive feedback are always nice, you don't need them to proceed. The phrase "I've got this" exemplifies the attitude of "I am enough." "I am enough" is not arrogance. "I am enough" is not "I am better than everyone else." "I am enough" means, whatever happens, you know you will be okay, thanks to your inherent value as a human being and the personal and professional tools you've brought to the situation.

Believing you are enough is an admittedly tricky concept to embrace! It's a concept I still struggle with every day. However, it's the underlying foundation required to bring Clown Presence to your presentations. Not believing I was enough was my mistake when I tried to save the show. I did not have enough confidence to reveal my authentic self and instead turned to artificial attempts to manipulate the audience—attempts that failed miserably.

Realizing that you are enough allows you to be more fluid in your interactions with your audience. If you're delivering negative news to a team, accepting that you're enough enables you to focus on their need to be heard rather than on your own need to be liked and accepted. You can validate yourself rather than rely on your audience for validation. You can see audience interaction as a gift rather than an interruption.

This is not to say that having confidence makes preparing your presentation less critical. Excellent preparation is the minimum expectation for reaching Clown Presence, as we'll see in the next chapter. But first, a more foundational view is required to prepare for connecting with your audience in this profound way. You must realize that you are enough.

The Joy of Connection

Even knowing that you are enough, you might still ask how anyone could attempt such an inherently anxiety-provoking exercise as "Save the Show." Why would anyone do something like that? The answer lies in the perspective of the Clown.

The Clown experiences life in a heightened state, motivated at the deepest level by the pure joy of connecting with and responding to the audience. As described in chapter one, the Clown term for this state of being is *le jeu*. When a Clown embodies *le jeu*, the performance comes to life. The Clown prioritizes this joy over any fear of the audience and has returned to a non-judgmental state of curious discovery and authentic reaction.

Audiences are mesmerized by this vulnerable joy because experiencing this pure curiosity and authenticity is rare. We are used to everyone keeping their defenses up. It's pretty refreshing to see someone being vulnerably human. We're rooting for the Clown. We actually wish we could express more of that vulnerable joy in our own life.

You can bring this energy of *le jeu* to your presentations by reframing your experience. Almost everyone feels nervous before a presentation, just ask Andrea Bocelli! *Le jeu* means consciously acknowledging that nervousness and then reframing it as excitement. Try considering the nerves as anticipation for your upcoming connection with the audience. Once the presentation has begun, *le jeu* means continuing to regard the connection with the audience as a joy and a privilege. Your audience will respond by leaning forward in their seats, eager to join in the conversation.

It's important to note that you can find joy in this back-and-forth dialogue with your audience, even in the most serious of situations. A presentation is the moment that communication leaves your mind and becomes a living thing. Even if you're simply delivering a team status update to a group of executives, you can still find joy in your connection with that audience, and you can bet they'll appreciate it! As we'll see, meaning becomes a co-creation, led by you, the presenter. Finding joy in that mutual discovery is the key to finding joy in connection.

Growth Mindset

In addition to reframing to find joy in audience connection, assuming a growth mindset can also increase personal confidence. When presenting with a growth mindset, you see potential hiccups or blunders as opportunities because you believe that change and improvement are possible. You believe that the presentations you make are a self-correcting process over time. Therefore, you focus on possibilities for self-improvement rather than what the audience thinks of you. You are confident that you are consistently getting better.

The opposite of a growth mindset is a fixed mindset. With a fixed mindset, you believe that you are born with a set level of ability, so you avoid any risks or opportunities for mistakes at all costs, like public speaking! Essentially, you focus on what your audience thinks of you rather than how you feel about yourself and opportunities for improvement.

Adopting a growth mindset has been shown to result in more positive outcomes. Psychologist Dr. Carol Dweck originally defined growth and fixed mindsets in her book *Mindset: The New Psychology of Success*.[6] In 2019, Dr. Dweck helped publish an additional research study delving deeper into the subject and found that high school students trained in developing a growth mindset improved their grades and increased overall enrollment in advanced courses.[7] Adopting a growth mindset works.

The Clown also lives within a growth mindset. No matter what impediments get in the Clown's way on their journey to connect with their audience, they never give up. The Clown always believes that change is possible. The Clown has boundless confidence when it comes to connecting with the audience. At the deepest level, the desire to improve connection with the audience motivates everything the Clown does. Mistakes are inevitable, but thanks to the Clown's growth mindset, they never stop trying new and creative ways to connect to the audience.

Building Personal Confidence

How do you develop the confidence for Clown Presence? Experienced speakers have learned from years of experience, but what about inexperienced speakers? It's the old chicken-and-egg problem. Which comes first? You don't feel confident because you don't have the experience, but you are afraid to get the experience because you don't have the confidence.

The secret is incremental progress by focusing only on the next presentation rather than becoming overwhelmed by focusing on perfection. Progress requires gentle inward curiosity and compassion along with a liberal amount of rewards to yourself for incremental achievements. Easy does it! Our culture certainly celebrates the hard-driving pursuit of career advancement, but that relentless drive can become detrimental without intentionally caring for the person doing all the work! Here are some proven techniques to help build personal confidence.

Self-Care List

To increase your self-care and self-reward skill, I recommend a great exercise inspired by Julia Cameron's classic book *The Artist's Way*.[8] Take fifteen minutes and make a list of ten to twenty activities you loved as a child. This nostalgic activity can be a refreshing undertaking all by itself. You might not have remembered some of these joyful memories for years.

Once you've written out these fun, innocent, and "non-productive" activities, actually put a few on your calendar following scheduled incremental achievements. Finished your presentation outline? Doodle for ten minutes. Built your presentation slide deck? Take a hike. Added audience engagement to your quarterly update? Go for a swim at the local pool. Clown Presence is not only about strengthening your audience awareness muscle; it's also about building your self-awareness muscle. By honoring yourself, you begin to trust that you are a valid participant in your dialogue with the audience, giving them valuable insights that will help with their needs.

Get In Front of an Audience

I try to have all participants deliver some kind of presentation during every session of my public speaking classes. I've found that virtually all speaking challenges, including filler words, eye contact, and gestures, begin to improve on their own simply by delivering more presentations in a supportive environment. Regular practice puts a growth mindset into action because practice shows that you believe that change and improvement are possible. In this way, confidence is built not only by building your skill but also by building self-trust as you achieve a body of completed commitments to yourself.

To begin regular presentation practice, seek out consistent, low-stakes opportunities that allow for learning and experimentation rather than just focusing on a few high-pressure presentation sessions. Like the fail-fast concept related to agile project management, delivering plenty of non-critical presentations allows a speaker to try out new ideas and build skill and confidence over time. Put together a short presentation that personally interests you and explore these three low-stakes speaking opportunities:

TOASTMASTERS

Established in 1924, this well-known organization allows speakers to develop their presentation skills through regular practice, constructive feedback, and a well-built curriculum. Joining a Toastmasters club is a relatively inexpensive way to guarantee you'll be putting time towards developing your speaking skills every week or two. A quick club search at *www.toastmasters.org* will probably show multiple clubs operating within driving distance of your home. Toastmasters teaches a very structured style of public speaking, somewhat different than the style offered in this book. However, regardless of the curriculum, Toastmasters is a great, low-stakes way to practice adding Clown Presence to your presentations on a regular basis.

YOUR EXISTING SPIRITUAL COMMUNITY

Creating a five to seven-minute talk about something you're passionate about can be an excellent way to deepen your spiritual practice while simultaneously improving your Clown Presence. Often, church, yoga, and meditation communities are eager to host external presentations on appropriate topics. Besides offering potential low-stakes speaking opportunities, these environments can also be wonderful places to receive supportive and encouraging feedback.

LOCAL SERVICE ORGANIZATIONS

Local groups such as the Kiwanis and Rotary clubs and Chambers of Commerce provide great services to the community and provide excellent networking opportunities for their members. These groups often have a portion of their regular meetings set aside for outside, unpaid presentations on a wide range of topics. Depending on the schedule of the group, they may be grateful to hear your presentation and eager to book you quickly. Make sure to ask about the specific requirements of their speaking slot, such as time limit, topic selection, and technical capabilities (visuals and mic). There are even services that will attempt to book your presentation at multiple nearby service organizations for a small fee. A quick internet search should reveal what services are available in your area.

Find a Fan

Pursuing any challenging goal can be a lonely endeavor and keeping yourself motivated can be difficult. As you set off on your journey to add Clown Presence to your public speaking, having a cheerleader in your corner can do wonders. Support is critical. Find a partner you can count on to deliver positive, encouraging feedback, someone who can help you reframe your failures by focusing on the positive aspects, and offer to do the same for them. Consider booking a weekly ten-minute phone check-in with them where you both can share and provide encouragement for each other. Having unconditional support can be a critical motivator when times get tough, enabling you both to continue taking incremental steps.

Positive Feedback

It's easy to overlook the benefit of consistent, positive feedback in this world of constant focus on results and improvement. Constructive feedback can be helpful for short-term improvement, but if it's at the expense of positive feedback, burnout will eventually occur. Positive feedback helps build the critical foundation of confidence so progress can happen over the long term. When initially trying out presentation techniques outside of your comfort zone, it can be helpful to first ask for only positive feedback. What am I doing well? What worked best about my presentation? What did you enjoy the most? Hearing what you're doing well makes hearing criticism later much easier. There's a reason why the "sandwich method" of feedback—offering constructive feedback "sandwiched" between two pieces of positive feedback—is so widely used. When initially building confidence, consider starting with only positive feedback.

Watch Yourself... Gently

Almost no one enjoys watching videos of themselves delivering a presentation. You're not alone! It's so easy to press play and immediately begin ruthlessly picking out what you dislike about yourself. However, in my classes, I've found that having students observe videos of their presentations has proven to be the most efficient route to individual improvement. So, to avoid tearing yourself apart when you press play, some guidelines are necessary.

First, self-observation without limits can be a recipe for self-flagellation. Before you watch yourself, pick only one specific presentation element to observe, like eye contact, filler words, or pacing. Once you begin watching, there can be great temptation to simply create a list of all the areas you can improve, but do your best to resist this temptation. Creating that list while you watch yourself can be counterproductive and effectively discourage any further self-observation.

I suggest that you also task yourself with finding one specific thing you did well in your presentation. This seemingly counterintuitive practice can build self-confidence and a gentle point of view towards yourself. Plus, as you continue to observe further sessions, you will become more familiar with your inherent strengths so you can leverage them in your future presentations.

Say No

Taking on and completing commitments builds confidence, but you must also learn to say "no." I and many others struggle with harmful people-pleasing behaviors. Sometimes I say "yes" when, if I'd taken a moment to consider my ability to complete the request, I would have said "no." Although saying "yes" in the moment can keep others satisfied for the time being, this can build to over-commitment, resentment, and the failure to follow through. Consistent over-promising and under-delivering not only harms your relationships with others, it also harms your relationship with yourself by diminishing your integrity and confidence. Carefully consider your commitments and only promise that which you can deliver. Accepting and following through only on the obligations you can reasonably take on will build integrity and confidence.

Chapter Three:

PREPARATION

WARNING! Before attempting to connect with your audience with Clown Presence, you had better have your presentation absolutely well-prepared! As discussed in the previous chapter, this journey starts within you by building the confidence to realize that you are enough to begin to let go of your need to control the relationship with your audience. Now you move one step outward by developing the essential presentation structure and skills required for Clown Presence. Preparation demonstrates respect for your audience. You must know your content so well that you have the bandwidth to care for and adjust to your audience's needs in the moment.

Preparing for the Unexpected

I learned the critical nature of this level of preparation during a Clown show that I co-wrote and starred in for a large Los Angeles theater festival. I was to play the evil host while another Clown played my innocent, non-speaking sidekick. We would introduce various acts to the audience as an overall storyline developed through the show. My sidekick performed the first act: a beautiful, silent, and moving juggling bit where she had to engage deeply with the audience with her vulnerability and presence. Plot-wise, this was the essential act of the show as it established her as the protagonist. The audience absolutely had to end up rooting for her character if the storyline was going to work.

She would ceaselessly rehearse her juggling act before, during, and after rehearsals. She asked countless questions so she completely understood the audience demographics we could expect during our eight-show run. She clearly understood her objective in the act: she had to get the audience on her side, a particular challenge for a non-speaking character!

Finally, after weeks of rehearsal, it was time for the opening night. We all stood backstage, almost vibrating with excitement as we peeked through the curtains at the sold-out crowd. Then show time! My sidekick and I rushed out to start the show full of energy before the eager audience and I soon left the stage so she could begin her critical, poignant juggling act. The audience was mesmerized as she deftly performed her act. She had them in the palm of her hand. I stood backstage nervously, going over my lines, oblivious to what was happening on stage. Suddenly, full of energy, I burst through the curtain. All eyes turned to me as I realized I had entered the stage too early, effectively destroying the rapport my sidekick was developing with the audience. I had screwed up. I stood there paralyzed. In the silence, my sidekick turned to me, calmly took in the situation, turned back to the audience, and seamlessly incorporated my blunder into her act. Her poise enabled her to maintain her connection to the audience, regardless of my early entry. In fact, she adjusted her act mid-performance to use my mistake to deepen her relationship with the audience even more.

Opening night was a huge success, many thanks to her ability to react to the unexpected. Her patient and thorough preparation allowed her to handle my disruption easily and even use my mistake to get the audience on her side. In fact, she ended up winning a best performer award at the end of the entire festival.

When it comes to public speaking with Clown Presence, a similar level of preparation is required.

You must build a strong foundation for your presentation: audience research, a powerful intro and conclusion, efficient memorization, and effective rehearsals. With this level of preparation, you will be able to more easily drop into the moment during your message, transforming your presentation from a one-way information delivery session into a memorable two-way conversation between you and your audience where you can deftly handle everything from unexpected latecomers to surprising audience reactions.

Know Thine Audience

Effective presentation preparation always begins with understanding exactly to whom you will be presenting. It's really all about your audience; getting to know as much about them as possible before your presentation will enable greater ease in dropping into authentic connection with them during your presentation. You must answer these three critical questions about your audience when preparing to present:

1. Who are these people in particular?
2. What do I want them to do, feel, or know after my presentation?
3. What's in it for them?

Who Are These People in Particular?

Do your best to determine the broad demographics of your audience: experience level, age range, hobbies, culture, etc. You can start developing the Clown points of view of curiosity and compassion towards your audience well before you actually begin speaking to them. Pulling together this kind of data can be critical when making analogies or using humor because they require a shared prior experience for comprehension. For example, I've learned the hard way that much American-culture referential humor does not work with international audiences—not everyone has seen as many Will Ferrell movies as I have!

Forethought on audience background is especially important when preparing for question-and-answer sessions as it will be much easier to reference appropriate examples to which your audience can relate.

Beyond basic demographics, if possible, go a bit deeper with your background research, determine what is currently top-of-mind for your audience and if and how they've responded to similar presentations in the past. This research can help prevent you from inadvertently bringing up hot-button topics or rehashing already exhausted discussions.

Of course, if you're facing an audience of strangers, it can be more challenging to answer these questions. However, you can almost always determine values that your audience shares because they're coming to listen to your presentation! Bottom line, put the audience first during your preparation and you will have a much easier time building empathy and connecting with them during your presentation.

What Do I Want Them to Do, Feel, or Know After My Presentation?

Thinking back to before I realized the critical nature of this question, I'm amazed that I persuaded anyone of anything in my presentations. When preparing for your presentation, write a simple sentence declaring precisely what you intend the audience to do, feel, or know as a result of listening to you. Go beyond vague words like understand, inform, or help, and try to define a measurable outcome. Spell out what's next. Do you want them to sign up for a class? Add their email to a list for more information? Talk to their manager about a specific policy?

It's tempting to avoid setting specific goals to avoid the pain and frustration of not achieving them. In this case, do your best to hold this goal loosely in terms of achievement and don't beat yourself up. Simply having this statement in mind provides a measuring stick to use while creating every point of your presentation. If a point does not directly contribute to achieving this goal, align it or toss it out. Your audience's reception of your message depends on it!

What's in It for Them?

"What's in it for them?" is the ultimate measuring stick to hold up to your presentation. Why does your audience care about your presentation? After all, it's not about you and your needs. It's about your audience's needs. Show them that you care about those needs with every word of your presentation, from your intro to your conclusion. Keeping your audience's needs in mind while writing provides another measuring stick for every point of your presentation. As before, if a part of your presentation doesn't answer this question for your audience, align it or toss it out. Your audience's reception of your message depends on it!

The Effective Introduction

In addition to conducting thorough audience research, you also need to ensure that your introduction effectively hooks in your audience right away. Anecdotal research says you have thirty seconds to get your audience on your side, so make those thirty seconds count! I'm amazed when presenters I work with squander those precious seconds with bland introductions or thank yous to the event host. Use those moments to grab your audience and prepare them to be engaged! Here are four foolproof tactics to grab your audience fast:

1. Compelling Story
2. Surprising Statistic
3. Unexpected Action
4. Engaging Question

Compelling Story

The ancient art of storytelling has captivated audiences since the very first presentation, perhaps around a prehistoric fire. Your audience wants to hear about fellow humans overcoming great odds to triumphantly achieve their goals. The whole of humanity can relate! While compelling storytelling can take a lifetime to master, the "story spine" can be a functional, shorthand structure for building a story to engage your audience. It may help to begin with the end of the story and work backward.

STORY SPINE

1. Once upon a time… Describe the status quo
2. And every day… Establish the routine
3. But one day… Break the routine due to a want or passion
4. Because of that… Consequences and obstacles

5. Until finally... The moment of truth into profound change
6. And ever since then... A better routine has been established

Your stats and data may be solid, but a good story engages your audience emotionally, resulting in a closer connection between them and you as the presenter, setting the stage for true Clown Presence.

Surprising Statistic

Can you provide clear data at the top of your presentation that challenges your audience's expectations? "What if I told you that seven out of ten of our customers actually want to purchase even more products from us than they're currently purchasing? Would you believe me? Well, let me show you how it's true and what we can do about it." Playfully challenging your audience also sets the stage for Clown Presence. We'll delve more deeply into this subject later in the play chapter, but suffice to say that starting your presentation with a surprising stat followed by a fun promise is a great way to get your audience playing with you right away.

Unexpected Action

For some reason, presenters often forget that they have the entire physical world at their disposal to engage their audience with their message. There are so many more tools available than just words! Try using multiple modalities to begin your presentation. Try demonstrating a verbal example with kids' toys, nonverbally acting out a customer interaction, or asking the audience to stand up and take a breath or stretch together if the day is getting long. By breaking expectations, you're priming your audience to join your level of Clown connection.

Engaging Question

Finally, asking an insightful question can hook your audience from the beginning. Be sure to do your audience research beforehand so you can ask a truly thought-provoking question, rather than just a thinly veiled prompt transparently attempting to lead your audience to your call to action. You want to be setting your audience up for a dialogue, not preparing them for a one-way broadcast.

The Compelling Conclusion

Besides crafting an attention-grabbing introduction, the next most common challenge my public speaking class participants wrestle with is creating a strong conclusion for their presentations. I get it! Once you've made your points, it's easy to want to wrap up as quickly as possible to get out of the spotlight and sit down. However, that last moment with your audience is the one they'll remember, so make it count! This is the critical time to drive home your premise or call to action and leave your audience with your message foremost in their mind.

While there are many effective ways to conclude a talk, an easy and powerful way to bring your presentation elegantly to a close is to simply return to what you did in your introduction. If you told a story at the top, return to the story at the end. If you gave a stat at the top, give a related stat at the end. If you asked an engaging question at the top, ask a related question at the end. Returning conceptually to your introduction when you conclude your presentation brings closure for your audience, leaving them with not only your message but also a sense of completion.

Effective Preparation

In addition to effective presentation structure, functional preparation is also critical in achieving a confident Clown level of presence during your presentation. Here are some best practices for memorization and rehearsal.

Memorization

While it works for some presenters, verbatim memorization of your entire presentation is not as helpful if you plan on connecting with your audience using

Clown Presence. By relying on rote recitation, you can miss the direct connection and engagement opportunities that Clown Presence can provide. However, partial memorization provides a helpful level of speaker confidence, as long as you truly know your content inside and out and are ready to diverge from your memorized prose in the service of audience engagement. Partial memorization can be particularly helpful in these four presentation sections:

1. Opening
2. Closing
3. Transitions
4. Humor

OPENING

Memorizing the opening can be helpful for carefully wordsmithed introductions or verbatim quotations. The heightened rhetorical speaking style of Winston Churchill and Abraham Lincoln has faded from use, but carefully chosen words will always be powerful. Also, memorizing the first few sentences of a presentation can assist with pre-speech anxiety. With the introduction memorized, the first bit of your presentation can occur on auto-pilot as you get comfortable on stage. After the introduction, and once you've become more comfortable with your audience, you may find that the positive momentum will carry you forward into the non-verbatim portions of your presentation.

CLOSING

Another useful part of a presentation to memorize is the closing. Conclusions often contain a rousing and carefully designed call to action and inspirational message. This is a critical moment! You want to ensure that your carefully constructed wrap-up has the maximum possible effect. Having your conclusion committed to memory will ensure that your audience remembers the powerful impression you intended.

TRANSITIONS

Speakers often neglect to practice the transitions between their points during their preparation, and it shows! They can fall into a wonderful rhythm and connection with the audience during one of their bullet points only to lose that energy and rapport as they look at their notes or slide deck to remind themselves of their next point. By memorizing a transitional line between each topic, you can help smooth out those gaps and keep the energy and the audience engagement at the top level.

HUMOR

Finally, humor can be the most crucial portion of a presentation to memorize. Have you ever had a family member or friend start to tell a joke only to have them realize that they've bungled the setup so the punchline made no sense? Unless you intend to make yourself the joke, getting joke verbiage and timing precisely right is critical in getting the laugh. It takes a strong sense of confidence to pull off written humor in a presentation successfully, so use with care!

Practice, Practice, Practice

Once you've memorized the critical elements of your presentation, it's time for repetitive rehearsals. Fun, right? Rehearsing may not be the most exciting part of public speaking, but if you intend to connect with your audience at the level of Clown, you must get yourself absolutely comfortable with your presentation. If you aren't confident with your presentation without an audience, adding an audience will definitely not help! You need to know your content so well that you can pivot, adjust, or let go of it entirely to engage with your audience. How do you get to that point? Rehearse!

> "How do you get to Carnegie Hall?
> Practice, practice, practice."[9]
>
> —*Unknown*

When I was hired for my first professional Clown job on the North American tour of Spiegelworld's Empire, I felt completely overwhelmed. I would be acting as one-half of the Clown duo responsible for hosting a nightly contemporary circus show in an 800-person tent from a tiny eight-foot stage directly in the center of the audience. My Clown partner and I would be responsible for performing funny acts, bantering with the audience, and generally keeping the energy up between the masterful contortionists and skilled artists in the show.

One of the Clown acts we were hired to perform was banana spit-juggling. And yes, it's as gross as it sounds! We had to learn to juggle bites of banana back and forth using nothing but our mouths while standing eight feet apart on the center stage. Unfortunately, banana spit-juggling was not yet a skill I had developed in my life. In fact, I had not developed any juggling skills whatsoever. I have always been conspicuously unendowed with hand-eye coordination. When I received the notification that I had been hired and realized that I had to learn this clown act, I felt terrified, alone, and utterly unprepared.

My partner Clown, blessed with a healthy sense of optimism, an extraordinary level of personal confidence, and a clear idea of proper preparation, suggested that we make a plan and focus only on the next indicated action. With two months to go before our opening night, we started meeting up at a local park for one to two hours a day with a fresh bunch of bananas, an empty trash bag (for the mess), and a good attitude (most of the time). My partner helped us be gentle with ourselves and I tried to observe my anxiety with curiosity and compassion rather than identifying with my fearful, panicky feelings.

At first, our task seemed hopeless, but only if I compared where we currently were with where we wanted to be. Focusing on only incremental, day-to-day practice made it much easier to stay motivated and positive. Even small achievements, like a volley of five banana spits, were deserving of a small reward, like a fresh coffee on the way home. As we improved, we occasionally gained a small audience for our practices. We even started to have fun!

Days went by, the incremental progress continued, and suddenly it was opening night. The lights came up in the 800-person tent as we stood nervously backstage. And then show time! Filled with wild energy, we sprinted to center stage and performed our banana-spit juggling in front of 800 laughing audience members! They went wild! We had done it. We had learned to spit-juggle bananas, but, more importantly, we had attained a seemingly overwhelming goal.

I could not have reached this skill level by constantly comparing myself to my ultimate destination. Simply focusing on consistent practice while gently observing myself with compassion was the way through.

While adding these elements of Clown Presence to your public speaking may not seem like banana spit-juggling on the surface, they will have a similar attention-grabbing effect on your audience. I've found that consistent, repetitive rehearsal is the quickest route to a confident and engaging presentation. Boring, I know, but it works. Getting the structure, transition, and words well-rehearsed allows you to begin to split focus between your presentation and the audience, which is critical in reaching Clown Presence. Here are five rehearsal tactics that I recommend:

1. Five to Seven Run-Throughs
2. Bigger Voice
3. Bigger Nonverbals
4. Public Run-Through
5. Tech Run-Through

FIVE TO SEVEN RUN-THROUGHS

A good guideline for effective rehearsal is to put your presentation "on its feet," from start to finish, five to seven times. Use your visuals and do whatever you can to replicate your presentation venue. For example, when I'm rehearsing to present on a loud trade show floor, I will turn on a loud news show in the background to match the possible trade show distractions I'll be dealing with. If possible, rehearse in a space big enough to move around as you will be moving at your venue. For example, if you will be gesturing to visuals behind you, have your visuals on your laptop behind you during rehearsals. Why five to seven run-throughs? I don't know the science behind it, but I can say anecdotally that six run-throughs are about when I know exactly where I'm at within my presentation at all times. I'm starting to get a bit bored with my content. Perfect! That's the ideal time to add in an audience that requires additional focus and care!

BIGGER VOICE

You'll want to close the door for this one! During one of those five to seven run-throughs, deliver your entire speech in the most variable and emphatic voice possible. Bellow like a giant during the hard data points. Whisper like a mouse during the thoughtful moments. Speak with a Dracula accent during the call to action. It doesn't matter! Just make sure that you are constantly playing with your voice's pitch, resonance, pacing, and volume throughout the entire speech. It will feel awkward at first, but after a minute or two, you'll find that your content and structure will dictate what kind of voice to use at each moment. While you'd never deliver your presentation in this manner at your venue, this exercise will push you out of your vocal variety comfort zone, giving you a more dynamic and interesting vocal presence when it's show time.

BIGGER NONVERBALS

Here's another tactic where you may want to close the door! If in the last tactic you were expanding your vocal variety out of your normal zone, in this tactic you'll be doing the same thing with your gestures and body movements. Begin your run-through by overemphasizing your nonverbals. Wave your hands to emphasize every point. Exaggerate your facial expressions to convey positive and negative data. Use your posture and move around your space to indicate transitions. Jump on your couch to tell a story! Crawl on the floor to deliver your call to action! Again, you'd never do this in your actual presentation, but you will extend the spectrum of communication tools you can draw upon to engage your audience. As a result, your message will connect more powerfully with your audience due to more integrated gestures, facial expressions, and movement. I've been stunned at the increased effectiveness of students' nonverbal com-munication after they rehearse with this method.

PUBLIC RUN-THROUGH

I've found this tactic to be the most effective method to prepare for my public presentations. For one of your final five to seven run-throughs, visit a public place with plenty of people, like an outdoor mall or pedestrian shopping district. Then take a stroll and simply deliver your speech aloud as you walk around.

I recommend wearing earphones so it seems as if you're speaking on your cell phone and not talking emphatically to yourself! I find this tactic a great way to prepare because I'm guaranteed to encounter distractions that will require me to stay focused on my presentation while reacting to the external world if necessary (be careful crossing streets)! This split attention is what we're looking to practice: attention to both your audience and your content.

TECH RUN-THROUGH

The final rehearsal tactic is to show up early to your venue and go through your presentation with as much of the event tech as possible. Stepping out onto a stage for the first time and gazing out into a vast ballroom from behind a podium can be intimidating, especially if one thousand people are staring back at you. If possible, arrive early and befriend the technicians so you can jump up on the stage and at least be familiar with the view (sans audience, of course). Chatting with your technicians will also allow you to completely understand what they require regarding microphones and visuals. Test everything you can and do a full run-through if possible: mic, slide advancer, laptop connection, projector, etc. Things can and will still go wrong, but you'll be prepared. Plus, you will have the presence to use those hiccups to partner more deeply with your audience, which we'll learn more about next.

Chapter Four:

PARTNERSHIP

How do some speakers utterly captivate a room? How do they seem perfectly in sync with their audience during every moment? How do they make their audience lean forward in their chairs with bated breath, simply by pausing? The answer: these speakers have skillfully established a dynamic partnership with their audience. They're presenting *with* the audience, not presenting *to* the audience.

In earlier chapters, you first developed your relationship with yourself and then developed your presentation. Now it is time to step on stage and develop your connection with the audience. What is the most effective relationship between you and them? In presentations with Clown Presence, there are no barriers between you and your audience. As presenter, you are not only aware of your audience but also authentically affected by them. In response, your audience is aware of and affected by you, the presenter. This dynamic, vulnerable, empathic connection is Clown Partnership.

Say, for example, you're delivering a presentation on your team's project status to a group of other team managers. As you begin your presentation, your awareness of your audience allows you to realize that they are clearly preoccupied—most haven't responded to your opening verbal greeting, some are checking their phones, and others are typing on their laptops. Utilizing the skills of Clown Partnership, you can drop your planned presentation for the moment and authentically and honestly check in to determine what your audience needs. Perhaps an urgent issue has arisen and you can help facilitate a solution before you begin or maybe your presentation should be rescheduled to give the situation the attention it deserves. You've shown your audience you care by acknowledging their needs. This care is what will make them care about your message. That's what partnership is all about.

Improv to Clown

My journey towards learning how to partner with an audience began with improvisational comedy.

I started with classes and then graduated to performances at improv theaters along the West Coast, including the Upright Citizens Brigade, the Improv Olympic, and Theatresports. Improv training begins by teaching students to partner effectively with their fellow performers on stage.

The foundational concept in improv is "yes, and..." which means accepting and building upon whatever your partner offers. Learning to give and receive this support transformed and changed my life. Improv hooked me from the first moment I realized I could bring an audience joy simply by supporting my fellow stage partners and responding to my impulses.

However, everything changed when I took a three-hour workshop on physical comedy. I noticed that the teacher, when performing a scene, would continually "check in" visually with us in the audience while simultaneously staying in the scene. I had never seen an improviser do that before! He would actually respond to our reactions. If we were laughing, he would laugh as well and continue what he was doing. If we weren't laughing, he'd try something else and check in again. Acknowledging the audience mid-scene seemed so risky and rule-breaking. I was stunned. I was also falling out of my seat with laughter.

Simply connecting with and being affected by us in the audience amplified the scene's hilarity to a massive degree. I felt like a partner in the scene, even though I was sitting in the audience! The scene became an echo chamber of engagement, developing a stronger and stronger partnership between the teacher and the audience. After class, I breathlessly asked, "What was that?"

"That," the teacher said, "was Clown." From that moment on, I had a new passion.

The Fourth Wall

Being able to connect and partner with your audience in this way is known as breaking the fourth wall. The fourth wall is a theatrical concept that describes the imagined wall in a physical theater between the actors and the audience. Imagine you're watching a play set in a kitchen where a mother recites a monologue all by herself. To retain the illusion of theater, the actor and audience must pretend that there is a fourth wall of that kitchen between the actor and the audience (in addition to the three walls seen on stage).

The audience must use their imagination to appreciate the play as written. The audience must pretend that they are peering in and watching the actual character alone in the kitchen, even though they know they are actually observing an actor on a stage. The fourth wall also requires the actor to pretend that the audience is not there. Russian theatre practitioner Constantin Stanislavski called this idea "Solitude in Public,"[10] or behaving as one would in private while actually in public. If an audience member sneezes or leaves the theater, the actor must ignore the distraction and continue as if the fourth wall of the imaginary kitchen was there. The audience is aware of the actors, but the actors must pretend that they are not aware of the audience. The fourth wall allows the audience to lose themselves entirely in the imaginary world of the play.

The presenter has a very different goal when speaking with Clown Presence. Rather than building the fourth wall so that the audience can disappear into an imaginary world, the presenter's goal is to do everything they can to utterly shatter the fourth wall. Say, for example, you're delivering a sales presentation to a small group of stakeholders in their conference room. Midway through your talk, another stakeholder apologetically enters the room, running late due to a conflict. Rather than stiffly ignoring the stakeholder's entrance, breaking the fourth wall could mean kindly and subtly acknowledging and welcoming the audience member to the presentation, perhaps assuring them that you can send them the material they've missed following the presentation. By acknowledging what is happening in the conference room and not calling out the stakeholder negatively, you have removed the fourth wall, reminding the audience that you are all participating in the communication together in that moment.

Removing the fourth wall draws your audience in because you respond to their presence, creating intimacy and establishing a vital partnership between you and them. Removing the fourth wall makes your presentation feel immediate, dynamic, and exciting. Removing the fourth wall demonstrates your respect and care for your audience. You are aware of your audience, and your audience is aware of you, which puts you in the prime position to partner with and be affected by them.

Clown Partnership

In its purest form, the Clown doesn't need a pre-conceived comedy act to achieve this level of partnership with the audience. The Clown's enjoyment of being present with the audience is enough, and the Clown immediately attempts to draw them into partnership. The Clown begins by making an offer that seems fun to do with or for the audience, like offering a flower to an audience member. If the audience responds favorably, the clown repeats and builds on the offer, perhaps by bringing out more flowers. If the audience does not respond favorably, the Clown immediately drops the offer. The joy of connection then compels the Clown to try something else to engage the audience in partnership. Perhaps the Clown quickly draws a sketch of an audience member and again checks for audience response. The Clown and the audience are partners in this journey of discovery, but it is the Clown's responsibility to keep the journey moving forward positively for all involved.

A classic Clown exercise teaches this balance of partnership and responsibility using the Clown's proximity to the audience. The Clown begins by entering and standing at the wall or curtain at the back of the stage, as far away as possible from the audience. The Clown then makes a verbal or physical offer for the audience. If the audience responds favorably with a laugh, the Clown can take a step forward toward the audience and try again. If the audience does not respond favorably, the Clown must take a step back and try something else. This structure quickly teaches the Clown to build a partnership with the audience.

As mentioned in chapter one, this back and forth between presenter and audience is called *complicité*. This is not one-way communication. If the presenter has successfully drawn the audience into the joy of connection, the audience actively participates and enjoys their direct connection with the presenter. Before *complicité*, the presenter tries to get the audience to understand the message. After *complicité*, both the audience and presenter actively pursue the same goal: a dynamic, mutually created understanding.

When the presenter and audience are in *complicité*, the respective statuses of the audience and the presenter are in constant transition. Who is in control? Who is running the show? The answer is it depends.

Who's Running the Show?

Control is shared in public speaking with Clown Presence. You are not alone up there! You and your audience are participants in a relationship. As presenter, you are responsible for setting up the elements of that relationship, ranging from tense antagonism to complementary partnership. Say, for example, you're delivering a presentation explaining an unpopular policy change to employees at your company. You acknowledge your audience as an equal partner by acknowledging the disagreement and perhaps holding space for alternative opinions if time allows. Remember, while they may not necessarily agree with your message, your audience wants to hear what you have to say. They want you to successfully present so communication can occur. As presenter, it is up to you to embody the elements required for an effective relationship with your audience. In Clown Presence, you want to share control.

Imagine a classic rally race, like the Monte Carlo or Dakar Rally. In these dangerous, grueling, multi-day competitions, a driver and a co-driver share the responsibility of getting each vehicle over the finish line. While the driver steers the vehicle, the co-driver handles navigation. If either of these roles is absent, the vehicle will not cross the finish line and the endeavor will fail. A similar relationship exists between the presenter and their audience. Both are essential for successful message communication. The presenter steers the conversation, but the audience confirms the direction.

While this can perhaps sound difficult and even precarious, there can be an element of relief with this partnership. Shared control means shared responsibility. Your job in the partnership is to show up confidently, prepare effectively and make connection a joyful priority so you can attain the subtle balance of control and flexibility. The rest is left up to your audience.

> "Faith requires that we relinquish control."[11]
>
> —*Julia Cameron*

This point of view is not a manipulative hack to more effectively persuade your audience. I'm suggesting a profound shift, putting yourself on the same level as your audience, setting the stage for dialogue amongst peers. By focusing on connection rather than control, space opens up, allowing your entire self to be present and partnership to occur.

Are You a Good Listener?

Bringing this kind of partnership to public speaking starts with careful listening. Most people consider themselves good listeners. In fact, a study of over eight thousand workers found that virtually all of them believed that they listen as or more effectively than their co-workers.[12] However, a commonly referenced anecdote regarding listening comprehension claims that the average person actually listens at only about twenty-five percent efficiency. Folks do not listen as well as they think they do! Bottom line: all presenters can use better audience awareness and listening skills. Listening is the engine that will power your Clown Partnership.

Vulnerability Is the Key

Beyond listening, this level of dynamic partnership requires allowing you and your message to be affected, changed, by your audience, and that means allowing yourself to become vulnerable. This kind of vulnerability can feel terrifying! It means acknowledging your audience's response to you and your carefully crafted communication.

Standup comedy is perhaps one of the most vulnerable presentation scenarios. Imagine a new comic preparing for their first open mic night. They spend hours carefully writing setups and punchlines that they hope will elicit laughs from their audience. Jokes have been crafted. Transitions have been rehearsed. Punchlines have been memorized. However, once the comic tells the first joke on stage, that preparation fades into the background. The response of the audience is what matters. How will they react? But more importantly, how will the comic respond to that reaction? The comic's response determines whether or not they will develop a partnership with the audience. Ignoring their response denies the audience and builds the fourth wall. But even with an unfunny joke, acknowledging the audience's response validates them, shatters the fourth wall, and can get them on the comic's side.

Being aware of and responding to an audience's response shows that you respect their opinion. Your audience may not agree with your message, but your presentation has become a dialogue of equals, where genuine communication can begin. Being vulnerable enough for this acknowledgment is the fuel of Clown Partnership, but this vulnerability takes confidence in your presentation. It takes courage to reveal who you truly are, which may mean acknowledging imperfection (which we'll cover in a later chapter).

Counterintuitive as it may seem, the more you allow yourself to be authentically human and fallible the more captivating you become. You have a responsibility to your audience to bring them not only your message but also yourself. Permitting yourself to drop into this authentic, two-way dialogue with your audience will transform your presentation into a memorable, engaging, and action-inducing message that could only be delivered by you in that exact moment.

> "Cherish forever what makes you unique, 'cause you're really a yawn if it goes."[13]
>
> —*Bette Midler*

Healthy Vulnerability

Being aware of and affected by your audience does not mean constantly adjusting your presentation to their whims. You must begin with a foundation of confidence and the realization that you are already enough. You must see audience response as regarding your presentation, separate from yourself; otherwise it can be tempting to take feedback personally. Don't do it! Seeking personal validation from your audience leads to an unhealthy relationship, not an equal partnership.

Healthy vulnerability requires an honest understanding of your motives for entering into a partnership with your audience in the first place. Why are you presenting? A goal of being of service to your audience rather than a goal of just getting something from your audience is critical. If you've developed the proper foundation for Clown Presence, you can partner with your audience with authentic, hopeful, and healthy vulnerability.

Empathy

Beyond the careful listening and healthy vulnerability that a strong foundation allows, you must also develop empathy for your audience. Empathy can be defined as the ability to non-judgmentally identify, connect with, and reflect the feelings of another. Empathy means stepping into your audience's shoes and seeing things from their perspective and background, which may be very different than your own. Without empathy for your audience, vulnerability can lead to resentment towards them if they disagree with your message. With empathy, you can listen and respond to your audience's needs and reactions to your message with compassion. You can hold space for all viewpoints and accept the humanity of all involved because you can see things from their point of view.

Becoming a Better Partner

So how do you begin to partner with your audience in this way?

It can be helpful to describe what partnership is not. A presenter who is not in partnership with their audience begins their presentation without any kind of audience check-in and immediately launches into their prepared points. Barely making eye contact, this presenter methodically moves through their presentation as if on rails, never once confirming understanding or checking for audience body language cues. As far as the audience is concerned, they could be watching a video recording of a presentation.

In contrast, a presenter using Clown Partnership immediately demonstrates awareness and respect for their audience through acknowledgment and perhaps an element of engagement. As the presentation continues, the presenter periodically checks in with the audience visually and perhaps with questions, gauging understanding and adjusting the presentation as necessary. Clown Partnership doesn't mean dropping unpopular presentation elements altogether but acknowledging misunderstandings and disagreements and engaging in an empathic discussion if time allows.

Building up the skills for true Clown Partnership in your presentations is not easy, but the payoff in clearer message communication and deeper audience understanding is worth it. Here are four ways to improve Clown Partnership in your presentations:

Improv Classes

Improv classes can help you strengthen your ability to be affected by and respond to your audiences. In fact, I've observed that basic improvisational training can indirectly solve a large percentage of fundamental presentation challenges, including filler words (ums and ahs), distracting gestures, and stage fright.

Improvisation is not about acting but about reacting. To learn improv is to learn to take whatever your partner gives you and confidently make the best out of it for both of you. By first learning to partner with your fellow improvisers, you will learn to be a better partner with your presentation audiences.

Emotional Intelligence

Clown Partnership requires an awareness of your emotional tendencies when reacting to your audience, as well as an awareness of your audience's emotional state. There are two competencies of emotional intelligence: personal and social.

Personal competencies have to do with your emotional self-awareness and self-management. These would include being able to recognize when you're starting to get flustered as well as techniques that work to calm you down. Social competencies have to do with your ability to effectively perceive and work with your audience's reactions. These would include recognizing when you've "lost" your audience due to an unfamiliar reference or unpopular opinion and techniques to get everyone back on the same page.

Emotional intelligence training helps avoid personal communication blind spots or misreading your audience. I recommend the book *Emotional Intelligence 2.0*[14], which contains self-tests and strategies for improving your emotional self-awareness and awareness of your audience.

Antagonistic Audiences

To build skills for handling conflict in your presentations, I highly recommend two books.

Crucial Conversations: Tools for Talking When the Stakes Are High[15] is a New York Times bestseller that provides a model for having a discussion when the stakes (and emotions) are high. It emphasizes being able to step out of arguments when presentations get too heated to refocus on shared goals while maintaining the critical connection and awareness required for Clown Partnership.

Nonviolent Communication[16] provides a communication model that removes the blame from heightened discussions by acknowledging feelings and needs first. This model allows for clearer, more compassionate, and more effective communication with your audience for Clown Partnership.

Hand Raise Engagement Exercise

Clown Partnership requires being aware of and affected by your audience. To receive a handy guide explaining and debriefing a fundamental exercise that I use in my classes to get speakers connected with their audiences, fill out the form at *www.doncolliver.com/wink-exercise*. When practiced with a few fellow speakers, this drill will dramatically increase Clown Partnership in your presentations.

Chapter Five:

(IM)PERFECTION

Bear with me for a bit of philosophizing. Premise number one: public speaking happens in public. Premise number two: to improve, we must make mistakes. Therefore, when we make public speaking mistakes, they will happen, you guessed it, in public. Yikes!

For many presenters, public imperfection is to be avoided at all costs. But have no fear. Imperfection is, in fact, the path to audience connection at the level of Clown. I first discovered this early in my Clown journey, where class exercises, like "Save the Show" from the Personal Confidence chapter, showed that imperfection is not only encouraged, it's essential.

The imperfection I'm talking about is when you authentically connect with an audience member but forget where you are in your presentation for a fraction of a second. It's when you become emotional about your topic for a moment before you return to your carefully rehearsed content. To be clear, I'm not talking about errors stemming from a lack of preparation or care, which shows a lack of respect for your audience (the exact opposite of Clown Presence); I'm talking about candid, personal, and imperfect moments, which can be your presentation's most powerful and memorable moments.

Presenting Imperfectly

Powerful and imperfect presentation moments remind me of my mother's memorial service. I flew home to Michigan from California to attend the event. Throughout the four-hour flight, I worried about how I would hold up emotionally during my scheduled short memorial talk about her. On the one hand, I wanted to be clear and direct in my celebratory memories of my mom. On the other hand, I wanted to be truthful and vulnerable before the audience and share my perhaps messy emotions. After all, everything I evangelize regarding Clown Presence revolves around authentically connecting with my audience. However, I also knew that letting myself become emotional in front of a group of potential strangers was frightening, challenging, and perhaps even impossible. Would I shut down emotionally and just shift into "get it done" mode? Would I dissolve into incoherent sobs? Would the audience be ashamed for me? I shared my doubts with a trusted and experienced speaker-friend and I was encouraged to move through the fear and generously acknowledge and share my honest emotions with my audience, both for them and me.

When the time finally came to deliver my thoughts, I did indeed begin to tear up as I shared some of my most treasured moments with my mom. My tears combined with sloppy laughter, full of the wide range of emotions that my relationship with my mom contained. I acknowledged my tears but didn't let them stop me from sharing. Following the presentation, many in the audience thanked me for my thoughts and told me how my sharing had helped them remember my mother. This sharing of authentic, imperfect emotion, rather than just sharing of carefully scripted words, was truly the most memorable aspect of my presentation.

My imperfection gave permission to the audience to use my memories and emotions as an on-ramp to their own, allowing us to connect on a deeper level.

This doesn't mean you should aspire to become emotional in all of your presentations, but it should encourage you that courageously revealing your imperfect self can profoundly connect you with your audience.

Clown Imperfection

While this authentic, vulnerable kind of public speaking simply embraces imperfection, Clown performance actually requires it. Imperfection is the fuel that powers a Clown act. In this classic Clown act structure, notice how imperfection drives the repeating pattern:

1. Clown enters with an optimistic plan to perform for their audience
2. Clown imperfectly attempts the plan
3. Clown vulnerably acknowledges the imperfection to the audience
4. Clown optimistically makes another attempt but fails even more extravagantly
5. Clown again vulnerably acknowledges the imperfection to the audience
6. This pattern repeats into greater and greater chaos
7. Clown accidentally stumbles into an unintended, surprising, and sublime ending
8. Clown exits

Take away the Clown act element from the structure above, and you're left with this:

1. Optimism
2. Risk
3. Imperfection
4. Vulnerability
5. Return to 1

In this Clown structure, the laughs (and tension) progressively increase during the heightening repetitive patterns, building to a release of laughter and tension during the surprising ending. The imperfection allows the audience to relate to the humanity of the Clown. Everyone can remember a time when they optimistically aspired to greatness yet missed the mark. Audiences aspire to be able to acknowledge imperfection yet maintain optimism.

During this act, the Clown acknowledges and owns their imperfection before the audience then bravely continues. When the audience sees that the Clown is aware that the Clown is imperfect, the audience is given permission to laugh. The audience is no longer worried that the performer is unaware of their imperfection. Owning the imperfection makes the performance feel safe for the audience because the performer shows the audience that the performer knows exactly what they are doing. This acknowledgment, relatability, and connection are the critical points to apply to public speaking.

Science and Imperfection

Social psychologist Richard Wiseman conducted an experiment investigating this connecting effect of imperfection for his 2010 book, *59 Seconds*.[17] He had two salespeople separately demonstrate blenders to mall-goers. While Salesperson A flawlessly demoed the blenders, Salesperson B consistently neglected to fasten on the blender tops before blending. As you would expect, salesperson B made quite a mess. After his experiment, Wiseman found that Salesperson B was rated higher on a scale of likeability. The audience revealed that they found it difficult to identify with A's perfect presentation but related to B's humanity. Imperfection can get the audience on your side.

> "Our most isolating experiences are also the most universal."[18]
>
> —*Steve Safigan*

However, these findings don't provide an excuse for lack of preparation. For a bit of imperfection to help connect you with your audience, you must start from a baseline of high competence. A 1966 study by social psychologist Elliot Aronson proposed a theory called the Pratfall Effect.[19] In the study, a group of highly competent and a group of less competent speakers delivered identical presentations. However, during their talks, some speakers in both groups committed minor blunders (spilling their coffees). Following the presentations, competent speakers who committed blunders were rated as more likable than competent speakers who were flawless. On the other hand, incompetent speakers who committed blunders were rated as less likable than incompetent speakers who didn't commit the blunders. Bottom line, excellent preparation is essential for Clown Presence.

These studies are not intended to encourage you to fake a coffee spill or a blender accident to trick your audience into liking you. Inauthenticity and manipulation are the opposite of authentic Clown Presence. However, honest, accidental imperfection allows your audience to relate to your humanity and see things from your point of view, provided you've adequately prepared for your presentation. A minor hiccup like a quick digression, a small technical gaffe, or a moment of forgetfulness can make you more relatable and your premises easier to consider, thanks to this uncoerced connection with your audience. Your audience empathizes because imperfection is one thing to which all of us can relate. In an exquisitely polished, sterile delivery, the presenter essentially disappears, becoming simply a medium of communication, like a video monitor or loudspeaker. However, if you seek to make your messages genuinely unique and unforgettable, you must bring your authentic, imperfect self to your presentation.

Perfectionism and Fear

But wait, I can hear you thinking, *doesn't my audience expect me to be perfect? They'll hate me! They'll laugh at me! They won't respond to my message!* At some point, all presenters have to deal with perfectionism and the crippling fear that comes along with it. First of all, I want to validate what you're feeling. Most speakers wrestle with the fear of imperfection daily. You're not alone!

When dealing with the fear of imperfection, it can be helpful to take a moment and ask yourself exactly why you are afraid. Then ask yourself the why behind that answer and continue to ask yourself why after four or five more answers. You may realize that you are afraid because you believe you are not enough. As discussed in the Personal Confidence chapter, if you don't already believe that you are enough, you'll be in trouble when you mix in some imperfection. However, if you have prepared adequately and have intentionally developed personal confidence, I encourage you to let yourself off the perfectionist hook. Imperfections and all, you will bring something to your presentation that no one else can provide. Your presentation may not be considered perfect, but it will be mesmerizing despite the imperfection. In fact, it will be mesmerizing because of the imperfection. You may even find your audience much more receptive to your message.

> "Do not fear mistakes. There are none."[20]
>
> —*Miles Davis*

Owning Your Imperfections

To enable the audience receptivity that imperfection brings, you must acknowledge and own your imperfections. Owning your imperfections allows your audience to move past them and remain focused on you and your message. In a presentation, unacknowledged imperfection can become distracting and even be ridiculed by an audience if it is not acknowledged and owned.

> "A suppressed laugh soon becomes a sneer."[21]
>
> —*John Wright*

Imagine you spill your glass of water during your presentation, which takes the audience's focus. If you do not acknowledge the spill to the audience, it will be difficult for them to return focus to your message following the spill. Admittedly, it can be hard to acknowledge what is going on "in the room" during a presentation. Acknowledging that something is wrong can be a terrible feeling. However, if you want your message to resonate with your audience, acknowledging what's going on is necessary. A simple callout of what has just happened will work, like, "Oops, there goes my water! Anyway..." This shows the audience that you're not only aware of the imperfection; you're also completely capable of carrying on.

If you avoid acknowledging the spill, you have created another, more harmful distraction than the original imperfection: the fact that you're pretending not to be aware of what's going on. This can create a break in audience connection, which can be fatal to your intended message. No longer does the audience care about the details of the presentation. Now they are focused on the imperfection and, more importantly, on your disengagement from the moment!

But by acknowledging the imperfection, taking ownership, and smoothly moving on, this imperfection can actually be a great on-ramp to deeper audience connection with your humanity. You could then create a pattern, referencing the shared experience of the imperfection throughout your presentation, highlighting sections even more dynamically than anything you could have pre-written. Perhaps, every time you mention a challenge to be overcome in your presentation, you could reference back to the spill, saying, "After all, it's just *water on the floor,* if you will. We can get through this!"

Admittedly, leaning into imperfection can be scary and hard! You have to veer from your carefully memorized script to address the immediate environment. However, if you are brave enough to vulnerably own your imperfection with skill and competency, your audience will relate and connect to you more deeply. Plus, you've been gifted with a shared experience that you can integrate into your presentation.

Dealing with Questions

Acknowledging what's going on in the room can also mean answering questions about your message. Ignoring confusion regarding what you've presented can have effects even more damaging than an unpolished presentation. Your audience can see you as pushy, out of touch, or unskilled at facilitation. In the world of Clown performance, ignoring audience reactions is a surefire recipe for a failed show. In the world of public speaking, dealing elegantly with questions is a critical skill for the health of your message and your relationship with your audience. Skillfully navigating Q and A helps everyone understand your material better and offers a unique opportunity to deepen your audience engagement. Here are six tips for handling questions during your presentation.

Be Curious and Compassionate

Shifting focus from formulating your answer to regarding the questioner with curiosity and compassion can set your response on a solid foundation. Asking clarifying questions and seeing things from their point of view will not only help you focus your response but will communicate to the questioner that you care about them. Intentional work on Clown Presence inherently develops this point of view towards your audience.

Take a Beat

Without taking a moment of consideration, audience questions can easily be misunderstood or even taken personally. Defensively responding as quickly as possible is rarely the most effective reaction to questions. Simply taking a breath or two to process the question before speaking can help you calm down and formulate the most helpful response. Don't worry if your pause feels like an eternity! What feels like minutes to you on stage can actually feel like mere milliseconds to your audience. Always pause and take a deep breath before responding to a question.

Consider Their Perspective

While you've probably already considered why your audience should accept your viewpoint during your preparation, it's also important to consider why they may not accept it. Predetermining your audience's probable objections and your responses is vital in preparing for their questions. When preparing your presentation, always ask these questions from your audience's perspective:

1. What is the downside for them?
2. What else is on their plate?
3. What is their next step if they agree?
   If they disagree?

Appreciate the Conversation

Receiving a question, even a question from an opposing viewpoint, means your audience is listening to your message! Engaging your audience in a two-way dialogue is the primary intent of Clown Presence, even if there is disagreement. Always be sure to thank your audience for their questions before responding.

Paraphrase the Question

It's easy to quickly assume a point of view behind an audience question and then respond to a question that wasn't explicitly asked. To avoid this pitfall, before responding to an audience question, rephrase the question back to the questioner in your own words and ask if you've understood their question correctly. Not only are you demonstrating that you genuinely care about their inquiry, but you are also helping the rest of the audience understand the question that was asked. Paraphrasing audience questions and asking for confirmation is a concrete way to deepen your connection with your audience.

Start with Agreement

Inevitably, most presenters face antagonistic questions at some point. When dealing with a conflict, be sure to follow the prior framework of starting with curiosity and compassion, pausing, considering their perspective, appreciating the conversation, and paraphrasing the question. At that point, determine and state the mutual purposes that both you and the antagonistic questioner share related to the issue. Finding common ground is a classic conflict-resolution technique that can start a non-confrontational, productive dialogue towards a positive resolution. Plus, it reinforces the intent of Clown Presence: connecting with your audience.

Getting Comfortable with Imperfection

Reaching ease with imperfection can be a challenge for hard-driving achievers, but the connection that Clown Presence brings is worth it. Here are some techniques to help you embrace your imperfection.

Meditation

Developing a meditation practice will help you build your ease with imperfection. The intent is to simply develop a detached, curious, and compassionate awareness of yourself. A ten-minute guided body scan meditation can be an easy intro to meditation. Before Clown performances, I always listen to a body scan meditation to calm my body and focus my mind for peak performance. Free meditation apps at *www.calm.com* and *www.insighttimer.com* have many body scan options to choose from, with various lengths, voices, and background music. During a body scan meditation, a gentle voice guides you to visualize consecutive parts of your body, one at a time, from head to toe or vice versa. Over time, this practice can strengthen your ability to observe yourself as a detached spectator, a critical shift necessary for Clown Presence.

Self-Compassion

When you make a mistake, a common response is to become frustrated with yourself and beat yourself up. Buddhists call this the second arrow. The first arrow would be the pain of the situation. The second arrow would be the pain you inflict on yourself by wishing you hadn't caused the imperfection.

In a society that focuses on relentless improvement, there is a surprising lack of acceptance of the imperfection that authentic progress brings. Accepting your imperfections can be seen as weak or a waste of time, but it's essential to make improvement easier. Plus, acknowledging imperfection allows for the Clown benefit of deeper audience connection.

Dr. Kristen Neff's excellent book *Self-Compassion* provides a simple exercise to develop compassion for yourself during moments of imperfection.[22] When imperfection occurs, Dr. Neff suggests simply placing your hand on your heart and then taking a breath to acknowledge and credit yourself for being human and trying your best. I remember doing exactly this in the story at the beginning of the Preparation chapter, when I, as Clown host, had entered the stage too early and shattered the critical connection that my non-speaking sidekick was developing with the audience at the start of the show. It took some serious self-compassion to refocus so I could finish the show! This practice works just as well to recover from an imperfection during a presentation, so you can reconnect with yourself and then better connect with your audience.

Stage Fright

Almost every student in my public speaking classes struggles with stage fright and fear of being imperfect in front of an audience. Me too!

A well-worn quote incorrectly attributed to Mark Twain reads:

> "There are two types of speakers: those that are nervous and those that are liars."[23]

—Unknown

Twain may not have said it, but that doesn't mean it's not true! To deal with those nerves, I do these practices before every presentation and Clown performance. Here are my four practices for managing presentation anxiety.

THE SOFT PALATE

The human body can naturally hold anxious tension by tightening up the soft palate at the top of the back of the mouth, essentially strangling the voice. One of the most effective ways to release this tension is also one of the easiest. A simple yawn does a fantastic and mostly involuntary job of loosening up a tight soft palate due to nervousness while improving your vocal quality.

To loosen up, simply induce three yawns before your prep sessions and presentations. For some reason, the human body often instinctively produces a yawn when it sees another yawn, so if you struggle, a photo of someone yawning will be helpful.

Another way to loosen the soft palate is to softly say the words "hung... ah..." three times. You will feel your soft palate lowering and tightening during the hung sound and then raising and softening during the ah sound. Warming up your soft palate in these ways will release nervous tension in your throat and get your voice ready to present.

DEEP BREATHING

I always begin my public speaking classes with a deep breathing warm-up. This exercise not only relieves anxiety around dealing with imperfection but also begins to warm up the diaphragm for optimum vocal resonance. This exercise is also beneficial for speakers who find themselves running out of breath before finishing their sentences.

> "Tension is who you think you should be. Relaxation is who you are."
>
> —*Unknown*

Start by placing your hand gently on your belly. Try to push your hand outward during your in-breaths by expanding your belly instead of your chest. Expanding your belly will lower your diaphragm, providing more space for air in your lungs. Once your hand is in place:

1. Inhale slowly for a count of five while expanding your belly
2. Hold your breath for a count of five
3. Exhale slowly for a count of eight while compressing your belly
4. Repeat

Try to do three deep breathing cycles every morning and before every presentation or practice session. As you become more comfortable with the practice, increase each section by three counts. Deep breathing prepares your body for optimal breathing and also transfers focus to your body from your stage fright.

VISUALIZATION

Another way to transfer focus from your stage fright is to take a moment before your presentation and visualize the anxiety present in your body as if it were a physical object. First, try to define its shape, being as specific as possible. This imagination exercise may seem like a wasted effort, but the imagining process creates detachment from your anxiety. Next, define your visualized anxiety's color as clearly as possible. Finally, describe your anxiety's temperature as accurately as possible. How does it feel in your body? Burning hot? Freezing cold? I have found this admittedly odd exercise to do a great job of shifting my mindset from powerlessly embodying my anxiety to observing my anxiety from a detached perspective. It will work for you too!

FOCUS CHANGE

Finally, intentionally reframing your experience can transform stage fright into excitement and the fear of imperfection into an anticipation of a deeper audience connection. See if you can shift your mindset from "needing the audience to accept my message" to "wanting to help the audience in the best way I can." This "being of service" mindset transfers your focus from your needs to your audience's needs, exactly where it needs to be for Clown Presence. This can hone your focus with laser precision, leaving less room for anxiety. Your audience will appreciate it!

Chapter Six:

PLAY

The epic journey to bring Clown into your public speaking reaches its pinnacle with Play. You started on the inside by developing your relationship with yourself; then you expanded to develop your presentation. After that, you focused on your vulnerable partnership with your audience and your comfort with authentic imperfection. Now it's time to push your presentation beyond the realm of standard public speaking and begin to authentically play with your audience. It's time to have fun.

> "I'm not that funny. What I am is brave."[24]
>
> —*Lucille Ball*

Play in the public speaking context does not mean the silly playground games of your childhood but rather adding an appropriate layer of playfulness to your presentation that reinforces your connection to the audience. In the realm of the Clown, audience connection starts and ends with play. A sophisticated speaker can bring this kind of play to every type of presentation, from amusing anecdote to serious oration, but the speaker and audience must share a foundation of mutual pleasure in connection. As presenter, you build this foundation of mutual pleasure by understanding and applying humor's surprising science and structure. Buckle up for a rather unfunny dissection of funny-ness! While "science" and "structure" are hardly playful terms, they lay the path towards the joy, connection, and engagement at the heart of Clown Presence. The result: a presentation your audience will not soon forget.

The Sneeze

Comedian Jerry Seinfeld meticulously writes and rehearses his jokes until he knows exactly how he will deliver them on stage, down to the exact length of his pauses. This is not Clown Play. A better example of Clown Play would be Robin Williams. Exploding onto the stage, Williams would start with a loosely structured set of jokes but would be aware of and willing to build upon any opportunities for play that revealed themselves. This created a dynamic, exciting connection with his audience that felt unique, vulnerable, and personal. This connection is also available to the presenter prepared enough to truly let go of their prepared presentation for a moment to take advantage of opportunities to find play in their connection with their audience.

My solo Clown acts often occur in a pitch-black theater, where the only illumination is a single spotlight on me, the performer. Darkness fills the rest of the environment, so I cannot see the audience at all. This can be a lonely experience. I have to work hard to generate connection with that invisible audience out there in the darkness.

However, sometimes, during a quiet part of my act, an audience member will make some kind of noise, like a sneeze. Conditioned from watching other performances, the audience expects I will ignore the sneeze and proceed with my act. However, if I break their expectation and simply pause and look towards the sneeze, I always generate a favorable giggle or a laugh from the audience. The sneeze, obviously unscripted, is an opportunity for me to interrupt my act and have some fun.

As my act continues, I can occasionally pause and again look towards the original sneeze, perhaps playfully blaming the audience for an imperfection in the act, and again receive that familiar laughter.

Why do they laugh? The explanation comes from the science of pattern.

The Science of Pattern

This bond created in play is based on mutually agreed-upon patterns. Humans are pattern-seeking machines. Patterns help us feel safe together. Finding patterns is how our ancestors avoided being eaten by predators. They learned through experience to recognize situations that had ended badly in the past.

This innate human response to patterns can also explain why some things are seen as funny. In 2008, evolutionary theorist Alastair Clarke proposed the Pattern Recognition Theory of Humor.[25] Clarke theorized that humor occurs when the brain is surprised by a change in an existing pattern. That change can elicit anything from giggles to guffaws.

Take, for example, the parent and baby's game of peek-a-boo. The parent covers their face and then surprisingly reveals their face to the baby, gently exclaiming, "Peek-a-boo!" A baby as young as four months old can giggle when the parent suddenly shows their face with a "peek." The pattern of the covered face has been surprisingly changed and humor (and adorableness) occurs.

Returning to my act in the black-box theater, a sneeze or cough during a quiet portion of an act is not unusual. The audience unconsciously expects me to react in a way that corresponds with their expected pattern of past situations where the performer ignores the sneeze. I change the pattern by doing the opposite: I react and give the person who sneezed a long stare.

Joke Structure

To further understand how the disruption of an established pattern can create humor, consider the standard structure of a joke: a setup followed by a punchline. The setup creates a pattern by setting up an expectation. The punchline surprisingly changes the pattern by breaking that expectation. Take this classic joke from the 1930 Marx Brothers' film *Animal Crackers*:

> "One morning, I shot an elephant in my pajamas. How he got in my pajamas, I don't know."[26]
>
> —*Groucho Marx*

The pattern or expectation created in the setup line is that Groucho shot an elephant while Groucho himself wore pajamas. Surprisingly, the punchline breaks that expectation by revealing that the elephant was actually the one wearing Groucho's pajamas. The pattern has been broken in a surprising way. Laughter ensues. And Groucho needs new pajamas.

Sketch Comedy Structure

A similar pattern-disruption-based structure exists in many types of sketch comedy. First, a "base reality" is defined, i.e. the normal, expected world or pattern that the sketch exists within. This base reality sets an expectation for how the world of the sketch would normally proceed. Next, an unusual thing happens in the world of the sketch and the world reacts in an appropriately surprised way, i.e. the "voice of reason." The unusual thing then happens again in a heightened way, followed by another heightened voice of reason reaction. This pattern repeats until the surprising ending. A sketch audience loves to understand the repeating pattern but be surprised by the specific ways the pattern is played out.

Take the classic "Dead Parrot" sketch from the British comedy troupe Monty Python.[27] A patron returns to a pet shop to take back a parrot that was deceased upon purchase. However, the shop owner refuses to acknowledge that the parrot is dead, regardless of evidence emphatically provided to the contrary by the patron. Within the base reality of the pet shop, the audience has an expectation that a dead parrot would be acknowledged and dealt with appropriately. However, the pet shop owner responds in surprising ways by repeatedly and creatively denying the parrot's lifeless nature, breaking the audience's expectations. Again, laughter ensues. But, alas, the parrot is still deceased.

Play in Public Speaking

So how do you use pattern and disruption to achieve Clown Play with your audience and how will it help communicate your message more effectively? Achieving this type of play even in the most serious of presentation contexts builds a bond with your audience, paving the way for the highest level of understanding and participation in your intended message. Clown Play starts with intentional engagement and heightens through pattern-building and breaking.

Acknowledgment into Engagement

Playing with your audience begins with engagement and engagement begins with acknowledgment. A 2010 university study examined students' attention levels during class lectures using individual personal response devices.[28] As would be expected, student attention declined as the lectures proceeded. However, the study found that when the lecturer would notice and mention something about an individual class member in the moment, all student attention levels in the class would increase. In your presentations, acknowledging something about your audience in the moment is a foolproof way to immediately increase attention and engagement.

For example, during your presentation, an audience member may nod their head affirmatively during one of your points. You could pause and emphatically state, "Yes! I saw that nod! This person knows what I'm talking about! Thank you, my friend!" followed by an exaggerated nod. Chances are you'll receive a smile not only from the specific audience member but also from the rest of your audience. By acknowledging that specific audience member's affirmation, you have not only engaged that specific member but also your entire audience.

Engagement into Pattern

To transform engagement into play, find or create a pattern and then surprisingly disrupt that pattern. If, for example, you've already acknowledged a nod of a specific audience member as mentioned above at the start of your presentation, you could create a pattern by giving that audience member another exaggerated nod later in your presentation.

Your audience will begin to expect this pattern, an expectation which you could then break by starting to nod towards the original audience member, then surprisingly acknowledging another audience member instead. You could also disrupt the pattern by jokingly inquiring why the original audience member did not nod affirmatively to one of your later points.

Finding joy in building these back-and-forth patterns and disruptions is at the heart of adding an element of play to your presentations. It allows pleasure in delivering your content and, more importantly, in the actual dialogue with your audience.

Clown Joy

It's important to note that all the engagement, pattern, and disruption in the world will not save a presentation without the presenter's joy of connection. The joy of connection is where Clown Presence truly differentiates itself from standard public speaking.

To fully understand how to achieve this pleasure in connection, it's necessary to return to one of the Clown terms introduced in chapter one: *clin d'œil*.

> "It was effortless. It was easy to play with these things. It was like uncorking a bottle: Everything flowed out effortlessly."[29]
>
> —*Richard Feynman*

The *clin d'œil*, or metaphorical wink to the audience, allows the presenter and audience to have fun and play together. This idea of a wink implies that "I know this idea is silly. You know this idea is silly. We both know that each other knows this idea is silly. Therefore, we can have fun and not take this idea too seriously." In the exaggerated nod example above, you and your audience both understand that you don't actually nod like that in your non-presenting life. Using a metaphorical wink, you've created a simple, playful pattern that you and your audience can share just for the duration of your presentation.

In my Clown bit in the dark theater, after I first looked towards the sneeze, I could repeat the look whenever elements of my act went awry as if to blame the sneezer once again. In reality, I knew that the sneeze wasn't the cause of my trouble, as did the audience. However, we shared a metaphorical wink that allowed us to pretend that this was indeed the case. Becoming comfortable with this playful energy enables you to have fun with your audience in a way that deepens the bond of play.

Starting to Play

Play brings all previous elements of Clown in public speaking together: Personal Confidence, Preparation, Partnership, and (im)Perfection. To begin playing with your audience, you must invite them to actively participate in your presentation via engagement. Here are some best practices for adding engagement to your presentations.

Acknowledge Them

As with the 2010 university lecture attention study,[30] the exaggerated nod example, and my Clown act interrupted by the sneeze, simply acknowledging what your audience is doing encourages them to join you in the moment and creates a sense of play. Be sure to acknowledge audience members positively, rather than calling them out for something negative. Simply mentioning what your audience is doing in the moment can elicit a favorable response and deepen engagement.

Make It Present

Another effective way to encourage your audience to engage with you in the moment is to ask them to use their senses. If you find attention waning during your presentation, simply acknowledge what is happening and then lead the audience in doing something together physically, like taking a deep breath or having everyone stand and stretch. Audience participation is a common technique in successful Clown acts for a good reason—it works! By reminding your presentation audience of their other senses besides their eyes and ears, they will be pulled back into the present with you and your message. Even having the audience find a specific page in a handout can move them from a passive to an active state, where you can more easily reconnect with them in the moment.

Tell a Personal Story

As mentioned in the Preparation chapter, stories are a well-known tool in effective presentations because they create empathy. The audience relates to the protagonist's wants, needs, and fears as they are brought along on the journey. Every successful Clown act builds a story and invites the audience along for the ride. By tapping into this shared humanity in your presentations, you can draw your audience out of passive observation and into human connection. Additionally, by using a personal story as an aside during your presentation, the audience can feel like you're breaking the pattern of your rehearsed presentation just for them, engaging them in an even more profound way.

Give Them a Task

The classic method used to engage an audience in play is facilitating an activity. Activities like sharing information with neighbors, switching seats, or even raising hands remind an audience that you're all in the room together, seeing and being affected by each other. Don't be afraid to add a metaphorical wink to your audience tasks, like making your worksheet activity a competition with the prize being the playful (and meaningless) title "Emperor of the Room for the Day." Adding participatory and playful activities to your presentation enlists your audience to co-create meaning with you in the moment, deepening engagement and connection.

Playing Better

Once you've attained audience engagement, it's time to play. Here's where you apply the creation and breaking of patterns to have some fun. These are ways of looking for and creating unscripted opportunities for play in the moment. Think more Robin Williams than Jerry Seinfeld. My recommendation for most presenters is to leave the pre-scripted jokes to the professionals. The safest target for humor is always yourself. Never insult your audience or what they love. Safe improvised opportunities for play abound if you can be open and aware, plus the fun will feel more immediate and connected to your audience.

Same, Same, Different

The Rule of Three is a cornerstone of comedy because it's the most efficient way to build and then break a pattern. At its most basic, the Rule of Three consists of reciting a list of three consecutive statements. The first two statements set up a pattern and then the third statement breaks that pattern with a surprising and ridiculous exaggeration.

In a presentation context, the first two statements could be earnest options for the lunch break, creating an expectation that the pattern will continue with similar serious ideas. "I saw some great lunch options outside: Subway... Outback Steakhouse..." Breaking that expectation by using a ridiculous exaggeration as the third idea can often get a laugh. "And if you're watching what you eat like I am, head across the street to the wheat field." Using the Rule of Three works great if you and your audience have an immediately shared experience from which you can draw.

Give 'Em What They Want

A classic Clown truism is, "If they laugh, do it more. If they don't laugh, stop." Your audience will let you know what they find funny. Being aware of their reactions can identify potential sources for repetition and pattern-building. If they laugh at something during your presentation, try it again at an appropriate time. If they don't laugh, don't do it again!

For example, the audience could unexpectedly laugh at an unscripted aside that you improvised during your presentation, such as, "I'll never do that again," "For which I'm eternally grateful," or, "I didn't see that coming." You could try repeating the phrase at other appropriate times: "I didn't see that coming either," or, "Something else I'll never do again." Be careful not to force repetition if the laughs have stopped. Trying to force a laugh can seem desperate and break your carefully built bond with your audience.

If... Then...

Another classic comedy truism is "If this is true, then what else is true?" This can mean taking some stated points in your presentation, considering them as a pattern, and then heightening that pattern to an unexpected degree with a wink.

For example, let's say that in your presentation, you propose that the solution to your stated problem is more research into the competitor's product line. So, the pattern you propose is that the solution to problems is more research. You could also mention that you have a problem watching too much Netflix. Heightening your pattern to an unexpected degree, your solution could be to research Hulu, HBO Max, and Amazon Prime for three hours every night!

It bears repeating that the safest target for humor is always yourself. If you're careful never to insult your audience or what your audience loves, plenty of opportunities for play can reveal themselves during a presentation if you are aware enough to recognize them.

Places to Practice

Learning to create and disrupt patterns in real time during a presentation can be challenging without practice. Here are two places where you can learn to play more skillfully.

Upright Citizens Brigade Improv Classes

The Upright Citizens Brigade, or UCB, is a well-respected comedy training school with centers in New York and Los Angeles and virtual class offerings at *www.ucbcomedy.com*. UCB improv classes move past simple "yes, and..." agreement training into actual, in-the-moment discovery and creation of patterns, as discussed in this chapter. UCB's curriculum brings great rigor and specificity to what makes an effective and humorous pattern and can be immediately applicable to finding play in presentations. While UCB improv classes are most effective, UCB's theories are also well explained in the *Upright Citizens Brigade Comedy Improvisation Manual*.[31]

Clown Class

Many different definitions of clowning exist, so I recommend a bit of investigation before joining any specific Clown class. The clowning discussed in this book is not circus-skill-based, which would be more focused on developing physical expertise like juggling or pratfalls. This book has explored Clown Presence: a heightened, specific state of being unique to each individual. Clown Presence springs from courageous vulnerability, confident authenticity, and the joy of connection. In this kind of Clown training, you will learn what is uniquely funny about the unadulterated you. Coming to terms with this discovery can be challenging, but embracing your authentic self can be transformative and incredibly powerful in public speaking. The Clown requires an audience to exist, so Clown classes work better in a group setting. However, Eli Simon's book *The Art of Clowning* provides clear explanations and sequential exercises for getting better at existing with Clown Presence if classes are not available.[32]

CONCLUSION

Congratulations! I hope that this book has gotten you passionate about transforming your public speaking through Clown Presence. I hope you're connecting with your audience more successfully than you ever thought possible. Implementing these techniques in your job presentations, volunteer speeches, and wedding toasts will allow you to show up before your audiences more easily, confidently, and effectively. Your messages will resonate with your audiences in more profound ways. Your audiences will find you more likable, warm, and engaging. Your dynamic, authentic connection will set you apart in the world of public speaking.

The Five P's of Clown Presence

We've covered a lot of ground. We started by examining personal confidence, which emerges when you realize that you are already enough, when you reframe nervousness as the joy and excitement of your upcoming audience interaction, and when your growth mindset embraces hiccups and blunders as opportunities. With incremental practice, you can move towards the confidence to truly connect with your audience.

However, proper preparation is necessary to connect with your audience at this level. Effectively preparing your presentation includes knowing your audience, crafting attention-grabbing introductions and compelling conclusions, and effective memorization and rehearsal tactics.

With proper preparation taken care of, you can begin creating a true partnership with your audience, allowing yourself to be affected by them on a moment-to-moment basis. You view your audience with authentic, hopeful, and uninhibited curiosity, confidently breaking the fourth wall with vulnerability and empathy.

You've faced your inner perfectionist and started to embrace your authentic, human vulnerability. By owning your imperfection, you're deepening your relationship with your audience even more and dealing skillfully with questions and stage fright.

Finally, you've taken this deep connection with your audience to the next level and actually started to play with them. By finding pleasure in the conversation by creating and disrupting patterns of play, both you and your audience are moving towards a mutually created understanding. You may even be adding a bit of a wink in your presentations!

You Are Enough

I hope these words have encouraged you towards a more powerful, vulnerable, and joyful connection with your audience. As you begin to implement these tools with incremental practice and self-care, be sure to solely focus on the next indicated action— one step at a time. But start now! Please don't keep your unique, authentic Clown Presence from your audience. The world desperately needs more truth and honesty and there's no one else who can deliver your message. You are enough. The world needs you!

> "We will express ourselves, and with this, other people won't feel so alone."[33]
>
> —*Charlie Kaufman*

WINK PUBLIC SPEAKING CLASS

Knowing how to transform your public speaking with Clown Presence is only the beginning! Putting what you've learned into practice is how you make it stick. If you've found this book helpful and would like to add Clown Presence to your presentations in the most efficient and focused way possible, please sign up for my next virtual public speaking course or book a class series for your company at *www.winkpublicspeaking.com*.

In this virtual class series of weekly two-hour synchronous meetings, you will focus on adding the elements of Clown to your presentations through intentional, fun, low-stakes practice. Topics include audience awareness, extemporaneous speaking, stage fright, executive presence, non-verbal communication, and presentation structure. As facilitator, I create a supportive, positive, and surprisingly fun space to push beyond your presentation comfort zone. You will learn research-based best practices and deliver extemporaneous and prepared presentations with personalized feedback. You will come away with a great support group and an increased ability to connect and engage with your audience at the level of Clown. Visit *www.winkpublicspeaking.com* to sign up. I hope to see you in class!

THANK YOU

Before you head out to deliver your next presentation, I wanted to thank you for purchasing and reading my book. I wrote this book to help people just like you and I'm grateful for the opportunity!

If you've enjoyed what you've read and found it helpful in building your public speaking skills, please leave a review for this book on Amazon.

I'm continually improving my curriculum and your feedback is priceless. If you've found a specific element of this book to be particularly helpful in your public speaking, I'd love to hear about it! Even a short one- or two-sentence review will help this book gain visibility so I can help more presenters connect more deeply with their audiences.

Thank you very much!

ENDNOTES

1   Elizabeth Hoffman Nelson, *Fools and Jesters in Literature, Art, and History: A Bio-bibliographical Sourcebook* (Westport, Connecticut: Greenwood Press, 1998), 246–248.

2   Jacques Lecoq, *The Moving Body: Teaching Creative Theatre* (New York, NY: Routledge, 2002), 147.

3   John Montopoli, "Public Speaking Anxiety and Fear of Brain Freezes," National Social Anxiety Center, February 20, 2017, https://nationalsocialanxietycenter.com/2017/02/20/public-speaking-and-fear-of-brain-freezes/.

4   Jerry Seinfeld, *I'm Telling You for the Last Time*, directed by Marty Callner (1998; New York: HBO, 1998), video.

5   Brené Brown, *Daring Greatly: How the Courage to be Vulnerable Transforms the Way We Live, Love, Parent, and Lead* (New York, NY: Avery, 2012), 34.

6   Carol Dweck, *Mindset: The New Psychology of Success* (New York, NY: Ballantine, 2008).

7   D.S. Yeager et al., "A National Experiment Reveals Where a Growth Mindset Improves Achievement," *Nature* 573, (2019), 364–369.

8   Julia Cameron, *The Artist's Way: A Spiritual Path to Higher Creativity* (New York, NY: G. P. Putnam's Sons, 1992), 56.

9   Matt Carlson, "The Joke," Carnegie Hall, April 10, 2020, www.carnegiehall.org/Explore/Articles/2020/04/10/The-Joke.

10 Constantin Stanislavski, *An Actor Prepares* (New York: Routledge, 1989), 82.

11 Cameron, *The Artist's Way: A Spiritual Path to Higher Creativity*, 193.

12 W. V Haney, *Communication and Interpersonal Relations* (Homewood, IL: Irwin, 1979).

13 Bette Midler, *The Saga of Baby Divine* (New York, NY: Crown Publishers, 1982).

14 Travis Bradberry and Jean Greaves, *Emotional Intelligence 2.0* (San Diego, CA: TalentSmart, 2009).

15 Kerry Patterson et al., *Crucial Conversations: Tools for Talking When Stakes Are High* (New York, NY: McGraw Hill, 2011).

16 Marshall Rosenberg, *Nonviolent Communication: A Language of Life: Life-Changing Tools for Healthy Relationships* (Encinitas, CA: PuddleDancer Press, 2015).

17 Richard Wiseman, *59 Seconds: Change Your Life in Under a Minute* (New York, NY: Anchor, 2010).

18 Steve Safigan, "Shame Resilience Theory," *Positive Psychology News*, May 16, 2012, https://positivepsychologynews.com/news/steve-safigan/2012051622128.

19 Elliot Aronson, et al., "The Effect of a Pratfall on Increasing Interpersonal Attractiveness," *Psychonomic Science* 4 (1966), 227–229.

20 Miles Davis, "Miles Davis Quotes," Brainy Quote, https://www.brainyquote.com/quotes/miles_davis_130826.

21 John Wright, *Why Is That So Funny?* (New York, NY: Limelight Editions, 2007), 93.

22 Kristin Neff, *Self-Compassion: The Proven Power of Being Kind to Yourself* (New York, NY: William Morrow, 2011), 49.

23 Richard Garber, "Did Mark Twain Really Say There Were Just Nervous Speakers or Liars?" Joyful Public Speaking (From Fear To Joy), May 12, 2020, http://joyfulpublicspeaking.blogspot.com/2020/05/did-mark-twain-really-say-there-were.html.

24 Stefan Kanter, *Ball of Fire: The Tumultuous Life and Comic Art of Lucille Ball* (New York, NY: Vintage, 2003), 8.

25 Alastair Clarke, *Pattern Recognition Theory of Humour: An Outline* (Beckermet, England: 2008).

26 *Animal Crackers*, directed by Victor Heerman (Paramount Pictures, 1930).

27 *And Now For Something Completely Different*, directed by Ian MacNaughton (Columbia-Warner, 1971).

28 Diane Bunce, et al., "How Long Can Students Pay Attention in Class? A Study of Student Attention Decline Using Clickers," *J. Chem. Educ.* 87, no. 12 (October 2010), 1438–1443.

29 Richard Feynman, *Surely You're Joking, Mr. Feynman* (New York, NY: Norton, 1985), 157–158.

30 Bunce, "How Long Can Students Pay Attention in Class?" 1438–1443.

31 Matt Besser, et al., *The Upright Citizens Brigade Comedy Improvisation Manual* (New York, NY: Comedy Council of Nicea, 2013).

32 Eli Simon, *The Art of Clowning: More Paths to Your Inner Clown* (New York, NY: Palgrave MacMillan, 2016).

33 Charlie Kaufman, "Inspirational Writing Advice from Charlie Kaufman | On Writing," BAFTA Guru, January 6, 2017, 17:31–17:38, https://youtu.be/eRfXcWT_oFs.

ABOUT THE AUTHOR

Don Colliver is a teacher, speaker, writer, and comedian with over twenty-five years of experience passionately engaging audiences and helping them engage with one another. Don's mission is to help every speaker profoundly impact their audience through the power of courageous vulnerability, confident authenticity, and the joy of connection. Thanks to his popular public speaking courses delivered internally at Google and around the world, hundreds of nervous speakers have transformed into more effective and joyful communicators, reaching a deeper level of audience connection than they ever thought possible.

In addition to teaching, Don can be found on the trade show floor, where he writes and delivers presentations for companies including Adobe, Cisco, and Medtronic. On the screen, Don has written and directed hundreds of hours of nonfiction television for shows including *House Hunters, $40 a Day with Rachael Ray,* and *Roker on the Road.*

Before teaching others to confidently take the spotlight, Don toured internationally as a theatrical Clown for contemporary circus company Spiegelworld and performed briefly with the Blue Man Group and he is listed in the Cirque du Soleil performer database. He is a founding member of the award-winning sketch and clown groups DJ Faucet and the Innocents. His troupes have received awards, including the Improv Olympic Del Close Award for Best Sketch Comedy Troupe and the Hollywood Fringe Award for Best Physical Theater, and Don won the 2017 Toastmasters International District One Tall Tales Speech Championship.

Don graduated Summa Cum Laude with a BS in Communications from Boston University. He holds certifications in Design Thinking, Applied Improvisation, and Instructional Design. He lives in the San Francisco Bay Area and when he's not helping speakers engage with their audiences more deeply, he can be found hiking through the redwoods. You can connect with Don at *www.doncolliver.com.*